JOINING the DOTS

the A-Z HANDBOOK for MAKING a SUCCESS of your CREATIVE SKILLS

ALEX MATHERS

*Thank you to everyone who helped me
make this book possible.*

ABCDEF

GHIJKL

MNOPQ

RSTUVW

XYZ

Introduction

Greetings, intrepid creative entrepreneur!

Thank you for choosing this book.*

Using our creative skills to make money and make an impact – while staying sane – can be hard as heck...

...If you don't know what you're doing.

There's a lot of information out there seeking to help creatives and artists find success. But much of it doesn't apply to people with 'arty' skills.

It can be dull, hard to understand, and at worst, downright unhelpful.

I know that people's definitions of success vary. For me, success is about doing what makes me come alive.

Every point in this book addresses this very human need, whether you work for yourself or in a team.

And if you're wondering, I do view one's ability to make money an element of success, even if it's not the full picture.

As an illustrator and writer with ten years experience building and growing my freelance business and helping others develop theirs, I've seen what works and what landed flat on its face.

I've been through the hardships of striking out on my own, including the pain of feeling isolated and lacking client work.

I've given the problems enough thought and figured out ways to fix them so that I'm now able to do what I love, love what I do, and get paid well for it.

Overall, I've learned that it is one's mindset, not so much the tiny technical details, that makes the greatest difference in determining whether one is a success at this or not.

Though none of us is perfect, how you think consistently will change everything.

This book distills into one quick read the approaches that have led to real results for myself and with the people I've worked.

I could have avoided many of the frustrations I've had over the years by absorbing even a few of these ideas.

Use this guide to align your thinking so that you can more confidently make the right decisions and make progress quickly.

The cool thing is that everything is in one place, to which you can refer again and again to keep you on track.

As the title of the book suggests, having these ideas in one place will help you join the dots, and see with greater clarity what it takes to be a successful creative.

Whether you write, paint, design, make things or help others do so, this book is for you.

I've included blank space with each chapter on which you can write your notes.

Feel free to read the chapters randomly, Z-A, or A-Z.

I'd encourage you to follow the Red Lemon Club newsletter for regular tips and articles from me about making an impact with your creative skills. Go to www.RedLemonClub.com to sign up in less than a minute.

The most important thing is that you get at least a few of these ideas imprinted on your neocortex and then act on them.

Your mindset coupled with actually doing stuff is crucial, so make sure you follow up each chapter by taking action, whether it's to move on to the next step or to learn more about it.

Let's start with the first...

---

* This is a collaborative project in which I wrote the book, Claire Powell made the fruity illustrations, Eugenia Cl ara made the hand-drawn type, and Jordi Calvet designed the book.

AUDIENCE

"*Good marketers see consumers as complete human beings with all the dimensions real people have.*"
— Jonah Sachs

It's easy to get carried away creating quality things that are fun to make, without thinking too much about who specifically your work is for.

Anyone and everyone who can get their grubby mitts on it right?

'My target audience is people!' you shout.

True, but not quite.

If you want to make money and make an impact from your creations, we need to know with greater clarity what kind of people are going to consume it.

Identifying audience was not something I did much in the beginning. My work was for anyone and everyone. The client work I'd get was varied, and many of the projects low paid and unsatisfying.

It wasn't until I started thinking consciously about who would benefit from my artwork and how I could mould my work and my presentation to these kinds of people that I was able to

start being proactive about my marketing and get paid much more by companies that understood my value.

Choosing an ideal audience starts with understanding the value of what you are making and how it can improve other people's lives and businesses.

What kind of people will benefit the most from your work, and how can you improve it to help them even more?

Who would be willing and able to pay you well?

Which people do you need to stop focusing on, who waste your time?

How can you adapt your work to attract the buyers with whom you'd love to work?

Audience

Who do you need to talk to for offering your creative services, so that you both win?

You might think that working for a defined audience compromises the quality of your output – that you won't work as passionately for other people and the restraints that this poses.

But this does not need to be the case. You can still create outstanding, expressive work.

Working with a particular type of person or company in mind will channel your focus. This will help your creativity because you are working within limits.

When you do your research, and list everyone who could benefit from what you do, you will come up with a colourful spectrum of different people.

That's ok because this is the first step in narrowing down your market until you reach a specific type of client, who will serve as your focal point.

> At any stage in your career, you want to have a clear idea of the ideal client or buyer who would benefit from your skill.

> Yup, this means one type of client.

Being definitive about your audience does not mean that you will lose opportunities for working with other client types.

When you know who your ideal buyer is, and take action to attract them and people like them, you will have direction.

With this momentum, you will take more action, and you will get noticed more by all kinds of people.

Like a ship ploughing forward to its destination, it can pull other boats along with it too.

Examples of ideal clients/buyers/end users:

* Recently funded technology startups
* Fashion magazines
* British male teenagers
* Accounting firms in Singapore
* Sports apparel businesses
* Fruit juice shops in New York

Start somewhere. Your ideal customer can be changed over time.

The more feedback you get from the market, the more questions you ask, and the more action you take, the more you will understand who suits you.

As Harley Davidson president, John Russell says, "the more you engage with customers, the clearer things become and the easier it is to determine what you should be doing."

When you know who is a good fit, you will know who to market to, how to brand yourself, what your ideal products should be, and how to expand to other, similar clients from there.

Knowing your primary audience will give you the direction you need with each step.

NOTES

NOTES

BRAND

"A brand is no longer what we tell the consumer it is.
It is what consumers tell each other it is."
— Scott Cook

A brand is a combination of elements that together make you different from other businesses.

Yes, this could mean many things, but if you want to stand out, you need to understand branding.

You might think of a brand as a logo or a visual identity. It is this – but much more.

It includes your service, how you work, the product, the way you present yourself and the way you talk about yourself and your values.

All of these contribute to the idea other people have when they think of you. Getting into hearts and minds is how to take your business much further.

The more memorable a brand is, the more likely people will be to remember you and work with you.

Overall, branding for me is about being consistent in what you stand for and letting all the elements that make up your public identity, reflect this.

Whenever I share something new with the world, I ask myself how this affects the image people have of me, and whether it makes the image more blurry or more clear.

You need to be clear.

Branding expert Tom Peters echoed this when he said, "give the world a clear picture of who you are."

Hasn't our red lemon made a splendid job of branding his lemonade stand? He certainly knows how to leave a big red juicy impression on our memories.

RED LEMON
LEMONADE
£1

BRAND

I try to make every decision I make harmonise with the identity I'm fashioning.

My identity includes the audience I'm serving and the ideas I share, but also the colours I use consistently; being known for very visual content, and the values I communicate through my writing.

Whether you consciously work on branding yourself or not, everything you show the world is communicating your brand.

When you think of well-designed computers, you might struggle to think of brands other than Apple. Apple is very conscious of their brand and work towards refining it all the time.

Even if you work for yourself, you want to build a brand in the same way that Apple shaped theirs.

This means being conscious of your story. It means developing an identifiable artistic style and voice when you write.

It's the type of client you attract and the kinds of reviews and testimonials people write about you.

All of these things will solidify your brand, letting the world know that you exist and mean business.

Overall, branding makes you memorable. It is this that you must strive for.

What brand are you building?

NOTES

NOTES

CHALLENGE

"*The ultimate measure of a man is not where he stands in moments of comfort and convenience, but where he stands at times of challenge and controversy.*"
— Martin Luther King, Jr.

The real pros know the power of setting up challenges.

You too need to set up challenges that require you to push beyond what is comfortable.

Is it not silly to set up challenges when running a business is hard enough?

Well here's the thing that I've found over years of running my life and working with hundreds of other creative people...

Success, growth and ultimately happiness will come to those who seek out and overcome challenges.

Challenges which you overcome, even if you are 'unsuccessful' the first or even the tenth time, means you are improving and growing. When you push for your business to grow, you are actively rejecting a comfortable and ultimately vulnerable business.

Challenge yourself by aiming high, doing more of what is uncomfortable but ultimately beneficial, and doing what others around you refuse to do.

CHALLENGE

In my writing, I'm always setting up challenges to write a certain number of words in an hour, finish books, publish a set number of posts each week and write on topics that make me think in new ways.

You can set yourself timed challenges to test and motivate yourself, like completing a project within a week, when you might have planned to do it in a month.

I always encourage my coaching clients, for example, to seek out bigger clients. Why settle for mediocre clients, and then complain about working with crappy people?

Now don't get me wrong here. I'm not just talking about big challenges that take weeks or months. I'm also talking about those daily challenges that lead to consistency in your creative output.

Writing 1000 words every day, whether you feel like it or not, is a challenge, for most.

Drawing a picture might be fun, but sharing a new one online daily for a year is a challenge.

Reaching out to one new person every day to expand your network is not easy – doing it every day even harder.

They're hard, but think of what your life would look like had you done those things daily, no matter what over the last year.

The things worth doing rarely feel easy.

So, rather than following the route of least resistance, challenge yourself by aiming higher and making those tough decisions requiring consistency every day.

Being 'challenge-oriented' will energise you and reward you in ways you never imagined.

It took a lot of daily practice for our friend
the fig to get to grips with climbing
a mountain. He's used to falling under
gravity, not working against it!

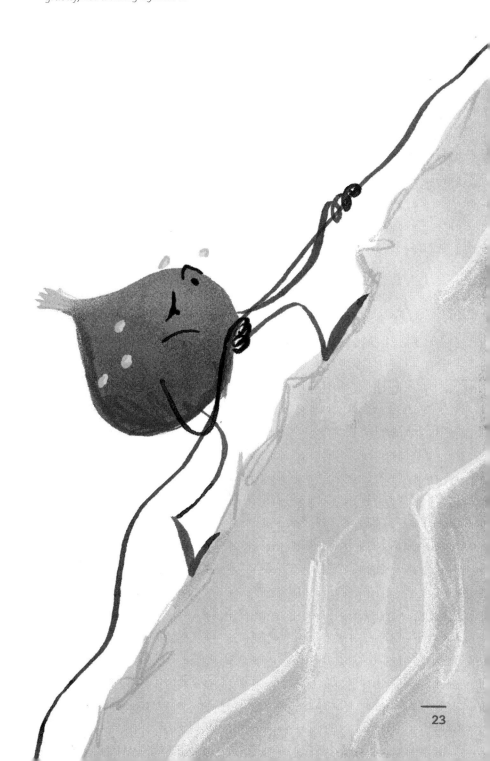

NOTES

DIFFERENTIATE

"Focusing solely on what you can do better than any other organisation is the only path to greatness."
— Jim Collins

I find it funny how much harder people make their lives by creating things that are too similar to everyone else's.

Differentiation makes everything so much easier.

Marketing lingo defines Differentiation as the 'process of making a product stand out as a provider of unique value to customers.'

Differentiation relates to branding, but according to my definition, the emphasis is on offering a unique product or service.

To differentiate is to see what other people in your industry are doing and consciously doing what they aren't.

Differentiation is adapting your product to the evolving culture and the changing demands that this presents too.

Your aim with differentiation should not be to compete but to dominate your market through doing what no one else would consider.

It's vital that you discover a corner of the market so fresh, so unique and so compelling that your ideal customers and clients would have trouble going to your competition.

It is a process that you need to continually work on so that you do not get left behind in an industry that is always changing.

Having a Unique Selling Point, or USP is one aspect of how you differentiate. A USP helps to uniquely identify you and promotes one unique aspect of your work that benefits buyers.

In having a USP, you are more able to demonstrate why someone should want to hire you over others.

My own Unique Selling Point as an illustrator has been my concentration on illustrated maps in my personal style, which no one can emulate without spending lots of time doing so.

There are also other things that contribute to why my service is a better choice than others that go beyond my USP.

This includes the influence of my geographical background, my ability to create detailed miniature scenes, my knowledge of online marketing, and my speed (sometimes!).

DIFFERENTIATE

All of these things combine to differentiate me from the rest.

Think about your strengths and what you can build on that clients would need.

How could you increase your value by becoming known for working in a particularly quirky style or a specific niche?

Differentiating yourself from others ensures that more people view you as the only option for their needs, rather than one choice among many.

NOTES

NOTES

EXCELLENCE

- -

"Excellence is not an aspiration. Excellence is what you do in the next five minutes."
— Tom Peters

Big economic crashes often tragically wipe out many businesses.

There are many reasons why some companies survive, and others fail. The factor that is always shared by those who survive is their dedication to excellence.

Being excellent is no longer a choice.

Excellence, in an age of the Internet, hyper-connectivity, transparency, and mega competition from talented people globally is a necessity.

Apart from dressing like our dashing gentlemanly pear, how do we become excellent?

To begin with, you must set high standards for yourself, for your brand, and for the quality of the work delivered.

Excellence applies to the full package: the product, but also to everything surrounding the work itself.

When you focus on excellence, and you stay true to those standards, your confidence will lift, and you will have the momentum to take things to even higher levels.

EXCELLENCE

Never underestimate yourself. There is always room to grow. Always set yourself goals that allow extra space for improvement.

Over-promise and over-deliver. Over-promise with ambitious targets. You should always over-deliver, whether with a personal or a client piece.

You must be determined to make each new post you write, and each new project you create, a little better than the last.

There is a difference between providing great work, and over delivering.

Excellence is not average. People expect good to great work. You must give more than is expected.

Excellence, combined with a differentiated product, will inspire others to want to recommend you and come back to you.

NOTES

NOTES

FRIENDSHIPS

"Our job is to connect to people, to interact with them in a way that leaves them better than we found them, more able to get where they'd like to go."
— Seth Godin

Having a healthy number of engaged followers, subscribers, readers, and fans is important.

It is your closer one-to-one connections, however, that hold the most power to make things happen.

I've seen this time and again in my own business.

Positive relationships create opportunities.

People like to work with other people they feel they know and trust.

They can also lead to real-life friendships that make working alone feel less isolated.

Much of business is about striking deals, whether through getting hired, getting featured on a blog or having a mentor agree to help you. As such, a successful business is helped by talking to people individually, building a personal connection, and making deals.

FRIENDSHIPS

Aren't our cherry friends having a jolly old time?

Developing friendships with people is your quickest way to securing more deals, more quickly.

One of the things I make sure I do each week for an hour at the very least is to reach out to people I know, and several I don't yet know, to continue or start a conversation.

Contacting people repeatedly will remind people that you exist and create opportunities.

They will come when you hang in there and don't allow a relationship to grow cold.

There is a whole range of great tools to promote your work and to get your products sold.

Use them, but don't ignore the value of one-to-one friendships to get more results, to sell and to land jobs, and to accelerate your progress.

NOTES

NOTES

GROW

"*The minute you're satisfied with where you are, you aren't there anymore*"
— Tony Gwynn

A sustainable business is a growing business, not a static one.

This might seem like a simple concept, but it is an idea that most business owners do not consider.

To stand out, to continue to earn well, to stay motivated, and be noticed, you must focus on growth.

The need to grow applies to the individual stone sculptor, as much as it does to a large software company.

Think of Andy Warhol and the help he got to be more productive and build one of the most recognisable names in art.

He would hire people to help produce more of his silkscreens more quickly, even commissioning others to help create products to sell under his brand.

He was dedicated to production over consumption, leading to a very visible, prolific body of work in the hands of hundreds, if not thousands of people.

GROW

He didn't succeed because he had a unique blend of wacky hair, passion and being a bit odd, though this certainly made him memorable.

He succeeded because he focused on growth and didn't stop.

One of the biggest mistakes I made was to think that my illustration business could remain small, with a few clients. Thinking small put a limit on where my business could go, and I was hesitant and uninspired to promote myself.

I thought that since I was a small business, what would be the point of promoting too much?

The inability to focus on growth is particularly a hazard for service-based businesses because you can only spend a limited amount of time on each project.

Aim big, and aim to scale things up.

The first element in this is to seek bigger and better clients, then to create new income streams. Sell products as well as your services, and scale things up.

It's easier to be motivated to sell more if you have the capacity to sell more.

I have supplemented my illustration income with sales of books and courses over the years, and it has helped free up time and to stay focused on creating and growing.

Look also for ways to create more. Creative output shared—whether paid or not—will contribute to being seen, and it will lead to improving and mastering your skills.

Are there ways you can licence your work repeatedly for a fee?

Can you collaborate with someone to produce something more quickly that you can sell?

Are there tasks you do that you could delegate that would free you up to do more of what you're good at?

Business is like wading upstream, and the flow of the river is reality and life's obstacles.

You will be swept downstream if you stand still.

If you walk at a slow pace, you will remain where you are.

If you strive forcefully forward—focused on growing—you will make ground, and you will stand out.

NOTES

NOTES

HONESTY

■ - ■ - ■ - ■ - ■ - ■ - ■ - ■ - ■ - ■ - ■ - ■ - ■ - ■ - ■ - ■

"Vulnerability is about showing up and being seen. It's tough to do that when we're terrified about what people might see or think."
— Brené Brown

In a connected world, in which everything we share is open to scrutiny, the value of honesty is now greater than ever.

Not being afraid to show up, to reveal your flaws and to have a voice, are all valuable currencies today.

People value those who can assert themselves consistently and courageously.

Honesty will draw people to you, rather than put them off.

It builds character and defines your identity – both vital for a brand that is memorable.

At school, I was very reluctant to contribute to the class discussion because I was shy. It's something I regret, but it also taught me that having a voice is more important than how you use it.

Dishonesty does not necessarily imply being devious. It can mean concealing something because of fear, like when we resist asking prospects for work because we're scared.

Honesty is being direct in communicating to prospects, rather than skirting around what might be uncomfortable, such as talking about money.

It is sharing more of ourselves.

It is being ok with being rejected because we are true to ourselves and our vision.

Honesty means that we say what we believe, even if we worry that some people may disagree. Being polarising might lose you some followers, but it will gain you even stronger ones in the longer term.

It is about being honest with ourselves, identifying what is holding us back, accepting them, and working to fix them if they need fixing. And it is in our ability to say no, to projects and people who don't gel with us.

Most of all, honesty allows us to have a clear conscience, giving us more energy that would have been stifled had we acted in a way we did not agree with deep down or had we done nothing at all.

Don't you just want to give our pretty mango a big hug? But be careful not to squeeze too tight. A particularly huggable distant cousin of hers became a smoothie in one such incident.

Notes

INCOME

"Making money is art and working is art and good business is the best art."
— Andy Warhol

I'd be willing to guess you spend a fair amount of your time worrying about money.

We value money so much that we're scared to lose it.

Unfortunately, this caution tends to infect your business.
If you're focused on saving money, you direct your focus away from making money.

The number one reason every business fails is that it did not bring in money at a rate fast enough to survive and grow.

If you create things for income, you must bring in cash, and plenty of it, as a priority.

It's not about ability here. It's about a shift in your mindset regarding money. Making money is a creative act. There is no shame in it because it will allow you to thrive.

Think of money as a note of thanks for providing someone with value that helped them.

There have been a few times when I've come so close to giving up my business entirely, and return to work in a job I wouldn't like because I had not prioritised money.

If you don't have cash flow, you don't have a business.

Don't suffer the fate of so many creatives by taking the pressure off bringing in money – the lifeblood of all businesses.

Don't listen to those who say it is not about the money. The fact is that it is about creating art and it is about money.

Artists without an income will not stay artists for long.

Who has your money? How can you expand the amount you make? No job is too small for you if you need funds urgently.

When you meet your basic financial needs, you have the liberty to work more creatively with the dream clients you always wanted.

Barnaby the banana used to worry about money. Now he's made of the stuff, and he's as cool as can be.

NOTES

JAZZ

Jazz music lends itself well to improvisation – creatively flowing without an apparent plan.

People who improvise do the best of what they can in the moment, given the tools available.

Improvisation is a neglected yet vital skill in any business because the real world is not predictable.

Improvisation is the art of adapting, and at the same time making the best use of what is on hand while staying within an outline of where one is going.

"To succeed, planning alone is insufficient. One must improvise as well."
— Isaac Asimov

Planning is often considered critical in careers and business.

To a degree, it is a good thing. We need goals, and there needs to be a framework, but the danger lies in planning too much and becoming paralysed by preparedness.

You can never prepare fully. 95% of your preparation comes from how other people respond to what you produce.
And so you must be open to taking action, using feedback, and adapting as necessary.

When coaching clients, I'm always slightly amused by how much of a mental spin they put themselves in trying to make sure everything is perfect before starting.

There's only so much you can do before doing.

Improvisation is not acting chaotically. It is moving towards your goals by being productive, nimble and flexible.

Your targets may change too, but you are always moving, always driven, always tweaking based on feedback, within your broader goals.

There is a difference between meandering aimlessly and improvising towards a target.

NOTES

KARAOKE

At a Karaoke bar, our purple pear chooses his favourite song and sings over a backing track awkwardly.

He might be a little tipsy, and, surrounded by raucous friends, he might feel shy.

As he relaxes, he finds the words flow better, and his voice glides over the melody.

Eventually, Mr Pear starts to get creative, adding more of his flavour to the tune.

The song becomes his own.

The parallel that Karaoke has with making art is that even the very best creative work is rarely, if ever, original.

Karaoke is taking something that works (i.e. popular music in this case) and making it our own.

As Austin Kleon has noted, 'great artists steal'.

Especially when you are getting started with a new artistic style or product, you will inevitably be taking inspiration, whether consciously or not, from art that has come before.

There is no shame in this. Every form of creative output has a backlog of borrowed ideas.

Take what has already worked, but borrow what has clicked with you.

Steal ideas from writers you love to read, practice your favourite songs on your guitar, paint in the style of the artists that moved you.

Then, with regular practice and an accumulation of experience, you will start to hone a craft that takes on its own form.

"Start copying what you love. Copy copy copy copy. At the end of the copy you will find your self."
— Austin Kleon

There is no need to re-invent something from scratch, especially if it has not been proven to work.

Karaoke

People are diverse and interesting, yet we all respond similarly to similar things.

When we become aware of what things leave an impression on others, but especially ourselves, we can apply it to our work and avoid doing things that fall flat.

I copied ideas and elements from the illustrators I loved all the time when I first started out. If something jumped out at me, I'd figure out a way to use it in my own work.

It was one of the most important phases in the development of my style.

Borrowing from – and emulating others – continues to be important in coming up with new ideas, and allowing my work to evolve.

I also look at what others are doing successfully to build a business, and I apply it to my own if they make sense to me.

Other people's ideas are the building blocks of your own form of mastery.

No one else can connect ideas the same way you can because we all experience the world differently.

Though we can copy ideas, melodies, or brush strokes, it is our individuality that makes originality possible.

When we connect ideas that inspire us, we have the potential to impact others.

NOTES

NOTES

LEARN

"The future belongs to those who learn more skills and combine them in creative ways."
— Robert Greene

If you have a creative business, you are responsible for many things.

One of these responsibilities – if you are to succeed, grow and maintain a level of fulfilment – is continual learning.

When so many people are doing excellent work, and with thousands entering the market each day, you need to be one step ahead in what you know and with what you are skilled.

Gaining an advantage requires constant learning to deepen your mastery and applying it through action.

One side of this is your craft, product, or service. The other is your brand and marketing that product.

A painter with an understanding of marketing is theoretically more valuable than one who lacks it.

LEARN

Regardless of what skill you're working on, whether doing your admin, honing your art style or marketing your work, you cannot view your skills as ever being complete.

I make a point of reading several books a month, even in areas that go beyond my craft, and I try to watch new courses and techniques in classes and online as much as possible.

Josie wasn't just a pretty face. She was determined to be the best science fiction writer in all the land.

The sense of my brain expanding as I learn is motivating in itself. When I read, I frequently pick up at least one game-changing idea that I can apply immediately.

Learn widely, but do not let this be at the expense of developing value somewhere more specific.

Mastery is not an end goal. It is a process. Don't let your craft or your business stagnate.

I've been both an illustrator and a writer. I also enjoy learning about a range of things, but my primary focus is to improve my value as an expert on creative potential.

For others, it might be in making an impact on the world with your paintings.

There is a difference between doing your best and doing the best it can be done.

When you do and know 'just enough' you will slip into a sea of average. You will fail to stand out, and you will give up. I see this all the time.

Going for mastery through constant learning gives your business purpose.

You are doing things the best they can be done.

NOTES

MENTOR

"A mentor empowers a person to see a possible future, and believe it can be obtained."
— Shawn Hitchcock

Beyond your personal experience, the most helpful knowledge comes from people who have done similar things.

It's very easy to forget or avoid the ideas and advice of others. It is also easy to take advice from people who haven't had real experience.

The best and quickest way to learn is to emulate those who have taken a similar path to where you want to go. But they must have been in the ring and have taken the knocks. Usually, it's very easy to know if they are the real deal.

By learning from them directly, you will accelerate your journey to success more quickly.

But even more valuable in a mentor is the inspiration they give by showing you what is possible. They reveal to you how an ordinary person can achieve something.

Eventually, you may even surpass your mentor. In fact, you want to aim for this.

I always thought I had it all figured it out. But it wasn't until I got tired of repeating the same mistakes, that I reached out to

people further ahead than me. From asking questions, I began to see the tremendous value hidden in the real life experiences of others.

I was surprised by how many people agreed to help me just because I asked. Many never ask, and it's a shame.

A mentor doesn't need to be someone you meet in person. You can find their ideas and experiences in books, articles, audiobooks and videos.

We're very lucky to have access to so many of the greats, but don't forget those smaller guys that can give advice from their experiences too.

Find out how people you admire got to where they are. Steal their ideas (See Karaoke), incorporate them into your own business, and thank them when you get there.

NOTES

NETWORK

"Relationships are all there is. Everything in the universe only exists because it is in relationship to everything else. Nothing exists in isolation. We have to stop pretending we are individuals that can go it alone." — Keith Ferrazzi

The idea of networking gives many of us the shivers. Most of us just want to get on with creating and leave corny networking to the socially gifted.

However...

A well-linked network leads to a healthy, impactful and profitable creative business.

If we sell products or provide a service, or simply want to be heard in the world, people need to know that we exist.

There are two levels of networks. You have the larger mass audiences of social media followers, or subscribers and fans. You also have your one-to-one network of more personal relationships that we talked about in 'Friendships'.

Both will help your business grow.

We need strong connections with people at an individual level to win jobs, gain mentorship, make deals, get promoted, and get recommended.

At the same time, it's important to continually grow a broad audience of potential buyers, fans, and contacts.

These are the people who subscribe to your newsletter, follow you on social media and frequently check in to hear what you have to say.

The greater influence you have, the more opportunities, sales and impact your creative work will make. A significant, buzzing network is especially important if you are looking to scale up, sell products and increase your cash flow (See 'Growth').

To attract people to you and your brand, you need to be visible, and you need to lead.

Share your creative work, including bits and pieces from behind the scenes, like your studio space and sketches. But also share content that helps and entertains beyond the artistic work itself.

NETWORK

Become an authority on a topic related to your craft, with your unique voice. Serve your people with ideas that will improve their lives. Reward your followers frequently. Show them that you care.

These are the people who will work with you, rave about you and buy from you.

I've seen my network grow over the years through my blog Red Lemon Club. A lot of it is because I focus on being useful in an area I care about for which I have become known.

Being visible through sharing and leading, as well as staying in touch with people as regularly as I can, has brought many opportunities, from commissions and book sales to speaking around the world.

Such opportunities are all possible because I'm always looking to put a hand up, inspire people to follow, and reward them when they do.

NOTES

NOTES

OMNIPRESENT

"I have approached all my business enterprises with massive action. That has been the biggest determining factor in any success I have created."
— Grant Cardone

Whoever said you could stop promoting yourself after you've sent one email? Well, I'm not pushing you, but the killers go as far as they can with their marketing.

The one thing separating you from mediocrity and bringing you big success has not changed in thousands of years. Having a great product is important, but that's not sufficient by itself.

There are many people I've seen with mediocre products who do very well.

They do well because people know they exist.

They get themselves in front of the people who need what they create.

They continually strive to get out of obscurity – the darkness, and into the light by being memorable.

With more people shouting to be seen, this is becoming more important.

OMNIPRESENT

Promotion is one thing, but omnipresence is another. There is an excitement and a purpose I have found that accompanies a push for omnipresence.

Being omnipresent means being everywhere all the time. Obviously, this is not physically possible, but this is what you want to shoot for in your corner of the industry.

If you focus on a niche area, this might not be as hard as you think.

Get in the minds of people creatively. Be in as many places as you can be. With modern tools, this is becoming increasingly possible.

If you have a great product, and you know people will benefit from it, then you should see it as a duty to be visible. Don't fear to be intrusive if you've created something helpful, beautiful and useful, even if it is not perfect.

As a side-note, be careful that you do not use promotional tools like social media reactively. You need to get in, share, and get out. You can dedicate specific blocks of the day to do just this. Do not become consumed by it, or it will eat into your creative time.

I recommend that people concentrate on a single form of media, one that builds on your strengths – whether that be writing blog posts like I do, or doing podcasts – but don't neglect the other ways you can get exposure through other channels.

I share daily content on Twitter, Medium, Snapchat, Instagram, LinkedIn, Pinterest, Behance, Facebook, my blog and through my newsletter. I share what I need to quickly so that

I can focus on other things without getting sucked into the social media whirlpool.

Sometimes I'll build content-creation into my day when I'd otherwise not be doing much else, like taking videos for Snapchat in my walks through town on my way to the shops.

Get help, if necessary, to get your content shared across the web and even offline, so you can focus on what you do best.

Figure out ways for people to become conscious of you and what you create, and when you have momentum, push it with all your might.

Oranges are actually trained spies, though they have a hard time blending into their surroundings.

NOTES

Notes

Problem-Solve

"I believe that if you show people the problems and you show them the solutions they will be moved to act."

— Bill Gates

People give you money when you solve their problems.

Anyone who is in business for income is in the business of improving the lives of other people.

As artists, how to solve problems is not obvious. Solving problems as a plumber, software developer or designer is more clear. But this mindset does apply to artists too.

We can also think of solving problems as fixing a need or giving people that thing they lack.

You are either providing a solution as a utility, like designing a website, or you are providing entertainment.

Buying a painting or a sculpture provides entertainment (and increased perceived social status and investment value tied to the value of that entertainment).

Solving problems requires that you understand people and what they need, but most of this will come from knowing yourself.

Most people share the same problems, believe it or not, and your best source of knowing what people need is knowing what you yourself need.

The best creative work is done for yourself, within the context of what others need.

I know what problems my illustrations and writing solve, and I make sure I address them when I tell stories or have conversations with clients.

If you can provide a solution to a real need, you will draw fans, and will attract people who are willing and able to pay you well for what you do.

Solve the problems of others, and you will solve your own.

Notes

NOTES

QUANTITY

"Perseverance is failing 19 times and succeeding the 20th."

— Julie Andrews

Making your business the highest quality will help you make an impact. 'Quality over Quantity' they say.

It's easy to get very precious about quality. It's important, but it's not all there is.

Meet Quality's ugly, but secretly very saucy sister: her name is Quantity.

A lot of success comes from seeing business as a numbers game.

Practising and producing quality requires days of constant practice.

When I started out as an illustrator, I spent over a year adding hundreds of illustrations to a stock website. It was only much later when I started finally seeing sales trickle in and people coming forward to commission me.

Seeing success with the best clients requires finding and engaging with many, and getting rejected by many too.

If you do great work, some opportunities may come your way. But if you want to work with the best, and you want to catch

the biggest fish, you will need to get out there yourself and put in effort consistently until you make a hit.

Doing things in volume means being ok with rejection, lots of tumbleweeds, and becoming persistent.

Seeing results with writing a blog requires you to share content many times until you establish traction. Traction is when people start to take increasing notice.

There is what I call a 'zero-traction' phase at the outset, for anyone who has something new to share. You need to expect this period. It will be quiet, but don't expect attention until you have created and shared hundreds of pieces.

People will start to notice when you demonstrate that you are persistent and serious about what you are producing and will not go away.

As Dilbert creator, Scott Adams says, "repetition is persuasion."

NOTES

NOTES

REMARKABLE

---

*"The job isn't to catch up to the status quo;
the job is to invent the status quo."*
— Seth Godin

If your finished work does not make at least a few people smile, cry, do a double-take or say: 'wow', you have to work at it until they do.

There is no room for satisfactory or good work in a highly talented world. It simply has to be remarkable.

Remarkability means creating something with a little twist to make you stand out from the rest. Something that took time, care, creativity, awareness, and dedication to put together.

Remarkable work triggers a response.

The way to do exemplary work is through a commitment to mastering one area at a time. Remarkable doesn't come out of only trying harder.

It comes from the accumulation of many ideas and experiences channelled into something unique and then letting go into a creative flow.

Remarkable work comes from studying an area more deeply and seeing connections others do not.

Be careful that the work isn't just remarkable at a technical level if you are making things to influence or inspire an audience.

I have seen artists who make realistic illustrations, but make little impression, because they left out the final ingredient in remarkable work, which is in generating emotion.

The work has to mean something; to tell a story; to be a form of self-expression; to be inventive.

Every decision you make in your career must lead to the creation of this kind of work.

In the early stages, it will take time to produce remarkable things consistently. So take advantage of being unknown, create a lot, and practice when no one is looking.

More than anything, follow what brings you to life, and express that gusto through your work.

Remarkable gets you the best clients, repeat work, fans, followers and recommendations.

Outstanding content and products will do a lot of your marketing once people see it.

There are no shortcuts to making extraordinary things, but it will come quicker when you create your niche.

You have one life. Why settle for mediocrity?

NOTES

NOTES

SELF-AWARENESS

"Your visions will become clear only when you can look into your own heart. Who looks outside, dreams; who looks inside, awakes."
— Carl Jung

Understanding ourselves is even more important than knowing your audience.

The more we know ourselves – what our strengths are, what makes us passionate, and what our values are – the more fluid our work will be. Your audience will be drawn to you when they sense this awareness.

If we know what we are good at, we can focus on what we do best and deliver the best products. If we know what makes us come alive, it becomes clear what is worth pursuing, and what to avoid.

We learn a lot of this through experience. You need to take plenty of action and fail a little to know more about yourself.

It's not always easy to know what we want.

If you don't know, find the things you don't like to do, and avoid doing them. But only avoid them when you're sure you can't try to improve on that thing first.

Weaknesses are often strengths in disguise, waiting to be explored.

You may find that something you hated turns out to be something you grow to love.

For me, I always hated the idea of public speaking but having done it a few times, I now get a lot of pleasure out of it, especially because it is a challenge that often leads to great things when I step outside of what feels easy.

Acknowledging our flaws is important. If certain issues are holding you back, you need to be honest with yourself and figure out a way of fixing them.

Being more aware of your negativity is crucial because then we can be more effective at cutting it short and focusing on what is working.

Self-awareness is so key because it helps you pursue what makes you come alive, rather than doing things that drain your energy to impress others.

NOTES

TRACK

"However beautiful the strategy,
you should occasionally look at the results."
— Winston Churchill

The management expert Peter Drucker once said that "what you measure grows".

Was he talking about magic beans? Possibly.

But he was also shedding light on an excellent way to stay focused and productive...

...Which is that by measuring and keeping track of your key numbers, output tends to increase. Why?

Because it forces us to see what is important.

Because we know how things are performing, we can build on what has already been achieved, and we can more clearly visualise whether or not we are making progress.

Seeing improvements in numbers is motivating.

I've always had a terrible head for figures, but I enjoy the process of looking over them. It's motivating and gives me back a sense of control.

Most people do not track much, if at all. Tracking one or two things like the amount of money coming in each month or the number of newsletter subscribers we're getting doesn't need to be hell.

There are endless tools to help us monitor all our data in the form of software, but there is, of course, the trusty notebook and pencil.

Tracking combined with setting targets can be even more powerful.

If you have interesting targets each month and year, and you combine this with tracking the things that mark milestones along the way, you're in business.

Sheila always knew how far she'd walked until she ran out of pips.

NOTES

NOTES

UNEXPECTED

"Do not go where the path may lead.
Go instead where there is no path and leave a trail."
— Ralph Waldo Emerson

This is where things get really interesting. As creatives, this is where we can make the most of what we do best, which is to be creative.

Creative thought is essential for making decisions – but not only for your art.

The most memorable brands frequently do things you would not expect. They surprise you at each turn. By being unpredictable, they keep us fixated.

Being unexpected is similar to being remarkable. It is more nuanced than this, however. It is being remarkable, but being unpredictable in your actions and delivery as well.

You want to think of yourself as a magician as your run and grow your creative business.

You are entertaining your audience in your unique way. Your clients, customers and fans will be drawn to you when you captivate and create twists along the way.

Being unpredictable is what makes entertainment work.

Think about Richard Branson's Virgin air balloon stunts.
They were unexpected and cemented his brand as a household
name in the early days of the company. You can apply this out of
the box thinking with your brand too, even if at a smaller scale.

I often get readers telling me that I always surprise them.

Whether it's with the ideas I come up with through my
illustrations and writing, or the places I choose to live in,

UNEXPECTED

I've never been too predictable. Unpredictability creates interest in my followers.

Generating fixation in your audience is an art because it requires a balance between developing mastery in your craft, and being unpredictable at the same time.

If you've been trying to figure out the code for having an audience stick to you like glue, being continually unexpected is your solution.

It's a known psychological phenomenon, that unpredictability will grab attention because you're breaking and rewiring mental patterns. If we expect something, the brain will more likely ignore it, because it is 'normal.'

How can you be unexpected, particularly if you have a clear style?

1. Market creatively. Do something for someone they would not expect.

2. Over-deliver. Do more than the client ever expected of you.

3. Do what others in your field do not do. Most are not creative. You must be the black sheep, hell – the wolf.

4. Regularly upgrade your work and vary the content even if the style running through it remains consistent.

5. Package, present and deliver your work in a unique way.

Over to you.

NOTES

NOTES

 VALUE

I've talked about adding value to your business so that you are valuable to others.

Being valuable is important in motivating people to work with you.

But you must also know your value for the sake of your motivation. People often miss this.

Firstly, if your work brings you to life, there is tremendous value there. Knowing this helps when you get discouraged if your work is not getting noticed as much as it could, or if you're wondering what the point of creating more is in a crowded industry.

The value in being brought to life through your work needs to be acknowledged. The point of creating should always start with you.

Another thing I see frequently holding people back from doing and sharing more is self-doubt.

Value

We've all seen artists who make amazing things that people want to buy, but still doubt themselves.

They are not motivated to promote their art or themselves or to make more.

I believe this stems most of all from not understanding why what you create – or can potentially create – can be useful to others.

You might make amazing things as far as others are concerned, and you might love the process, but if you don't understand and acknowledge that you have the value that others want, you will doubt yourself.

When some thought is given to why your work is needed, no matter what it is you create, you might find more to like than you think.

This will help you bring it to the people who need it with confidence.

Fred knew he looked cool. He could barely lift his arms from the weight of his bling, but it was worth it.

Notes

NOTES

Winning

"*Winning isn't everything; it's the only thing.*"
— Vince Lombardi

I've seen a lot of people who decided to start their own business or write a new book or start a new painting, who just stopped. They never completed it.

What happened?

They just couldn't find the motivation to keep going because they weren't conscious of winning.

Most people sabotage their progress by letting the insignificant become significant at the expense of winning.

Less important things like...

- Spending too much time dealing with crap clients.

- Trying to plan everything.

- Worrying about money over doing things that earn more.

Succeeding is shifting your focus from the trivial stuff to what helps you feel good and win.

Winning

There are three parts to following a 'winning' philosophy:

1. Make a note of your wins.

Despite all the talk of needing to fail often, there are only so many failures we can take; so little progress we can see before we give up.

You will not be motivated if you do not strive for – and take note of – your wins.

Of course, you need to win in the first place, but often it's about how you frame things. A lot of us don't pay attention to our successes, especially the small ones.

We're usually too focused on what isn't working.

Whenever I remember to do so, in the last few moments before falling asleep at night, I make a note in my mind of all the successes I've had during the day, including the tiny ones.

Noting my wins never fails to lift me up, setting me up with good thoughts into the next day.

Simply thinking about these little successes trains my brain to notice and attract more winning.

2. Focus on creating more wins.

This sounds obvious, but many overlook it. I still spend far too much of my time worrying about the things that hold me back, rather than moving forward.

Generate more wins by creating a strategy that leads to more, like getting up on time, writing a certain number of words each day or sharing a few things each week on social media.

With greater confidence and a better awareness of what is working in your business, you must build on and seek out new successes energetically.

You do this with such enthusiasm that you don't even need to look back on those little things that got your knickers in a twist before.

For example, if you had a client project that was enjoyable and well-paid, then it's your priority to bring in more of this kind of work.

Seek the best projects out and scale them up. Then you won't even have to worry about all those clients who stressed you out and wasted your time.

3. Seek out win-win deals with people.

Always be looking to make win-win deals. You want to focus on your wins, but things will move quicker when you help others succeed too.

People will be drawn to you and want to help you more, like by recommending you and supporting you.

You need to tune into winning like a bull that zeroes in on red.

This applies to you and to the people you lift up along the way.

That's how people build great businesses.

They seek out wins, acknowledge that they happened, do more of what worked, and help others win too.

NOTES

XENIAL

"If people like you they'll listen to you, but if they trust you they'll do business with you."
— Zig Ziglar

Finding a word beginning with 'X' was challenging, but I was thankful to find 'Xenial', which means being hospitable.

People are more likely to do business with you when they feel welcome, and they feel they can trust you.

How you interact with clients; how presentable your work is; how credible you are and how straightforward it is to use your website, all contribute to a general feeling of trust.

I come across so many products, profiles, portfolios and websites that do not feel welcoming. The navigation on websites, for example, is awkward and the written copy feels too formal, impersonal and bland.

Think about how you would want to experience your website from the client's point of view.

Speak directly to your ideal clients. Rather than trying to impress people with empty words, show them how you are a useful person with a voice.

Seek always to provide value, rather than to impress. Trying to impress usually leads to overcomplicating things. It's something I have to remind myself of all the time.

If in doubt, keep things simple. People have limited time, so you want to make the user experience simple and enjoyable.

Demonstrate that you and your brand is to be trusted. Talk about yourself like a person would, with warts and all.

Tell us stories that demonstrate why you care. Tell us that you know how to solve our problems and want to see us succeed.

Show testimonials where you can, and show a picture of you and where you work.

Showing that other people get your approval is extremely persuasive. This is social proof.

Anything that paints the picture of you as a credible, authentic human being will help put clients and customers at ease, and you will more likely strike a deal or make a sale.

Rudolph always made sure guests felt welcome, even if he didn't wear trousers.

NOTES

YELL

All our lives, most of us have been told not to yell.

Parents, friends and teachers, often with good intentions, reinforce the idea that it's wrong to be extroverted; to speak highly of ourselves; to rock the boat; to push; to ask.

And so societal programming has created an invisible force field around each of us that stops us getting what we want.

A lot of the people I've worked with, myself included, often make excuses about self-promotion. Usually, it revolves around things other than the real truth of it, which is that we're scared about what others will think when we show ourselves.

If you have a great product that benefits people, you need to understand why you are valuable so that the product gets to the people that need it.

You must see success as a duty that requires whatever it requires of you, including promotion and strengthening your network.

You need to do this with all your energy, and you need to be ok with rejection because it is part of it.

I rarely feel like sending an email to someone I don't know, but it gets done because I have strong reasons behind why I need to do it.

Read about how so many of the most successful writers and creators of our time were repeatedly rejected, but followed up enough to finally land a deal.

Drop the programming, and take pride in yourself. **Be ok with self-promotion, even if it doesn't feel comfortable.**

Why put all that work into something if nobody hears about it or pays you for it?

Sharing lots of beautiful work counts. You don't always have to be selling, but you do need to be distributing your content when and where you can.

Talk to people, have conversations, push, follow up and ask for a deal.

Follow up until those who need your work say yes.

NOTES

ZEALOUS

- -

"People don't buy what you do; they buy why you do it."
— Simon Sinek

Last but not least in our alphabet is being zealous.

The Oxford English Dictionary definition of Zeal: 'Great energy or enthusiasm in pursuit of a cause or an objective.'

Seemingly passionate people do not always wake up in the morning bouncing with energy.

There are off-days, and there are going to be peaks and dips in their mood. And yet they work on getting what they want every day, or at least most days.

The big difference between highly determined people and the Average Jeffrey is not that they were blessed with more passion.

What sets them apart is that they have made a commitment to exciting objectives that guide them to act, regardless of how they feel.

My passion for what I do comes out of working at it, not because I'm a naturally passionate illustrator. In fact, I became one by accident, but I have been working hard to make something of it for over a decade.

Sammy knew that unless he wanted to
end up in the fridge, now was his only
chance of escape.

Zealous

I'm not always consistent, but I remind myself – as often as I can – why I'm moving towards my goals.

Persistent people know what they're aiming for, what they need to do each day to get there, and they have compelling reasons why.

Is it to be a bestselling author? Is it to develop mastery in your craft? Is it to help you become financially able to devote more time for creative work? Is it to inspire others through your art?

What do you need to do every day to become the person you want to be? What are the several reasons (there are usually more than one) behind why you must get the work done?

Knowing this is what destroys procrastination and creates the energy you need.

Every additional reason you have for doing something will strengthen your purpose.

Write down your commitments every day. I write out my longer term goals and my short term tasks daily. If I lack motivation, I write out all the reasons why I must continue.

If what you're doing does not regularly charge you up, clarifying your objectives will help.

If they don't, it might be a sign that you need to change direction to something that does.

That's ok because this is a journey.

If you have a good reason to take action and feel alive when you do, you've already made it.

NOTES

NOTES

About the Author

Alex Mathers is a writer from London, UK. In 2009 he set up Red Lemon Club, a blog focusing on helping creative people make an impact with their creative skills.

He is a also a self-taught illustrator and has worked on graphics projects with clients like Mars, Saatchi & Saatchi, Google, Dots Games, BBC and Secret Cinema.

Find more of his writing at www.redlemonclub.com.

About the Illustrator

Claire Powell is a London-based illustrator who has designed for Nickelodeon, BBC and DreamWorks Animation. She animated the award-winning short film 'The Scapegoat' and is now working as a children's book illustrator, represented by literary agents Darley Anderson.

Claire's debut children's picture book, 'How to Hide A Giraffe' was published in July 2017 by Simon and Schuster.

Find more of her work at www.claire-powell.com.

Follow Alex's ideas on expanding your creative potential and making an impact through the Red Lemon Club newsletter.

Sign up on the site:

www.RedLemonClub.com

Made in the USA
San Bernardino, CA
05 September 2017